Canadian Politics Unplugged

Canadian Politics Unplugged

Eric Nicol and
Peter Whalley

Introduction by
Stuart McLean

A HOUNSLOW BOOK
A MEMBER OF THE DUNDURN GROUP
TORONTO · OXFORD

Publisher: Anthony Hawke
Copy-editor: Jennifer Bergeron
Design: Jennifer Scott
Printer: Webcom

Canadian Cataloguing in Publication Data

Nicol, Eric, 1919-
Canadian politics unplugged / by Eric Nicol ; illustrations by Peter Whalley.

ISBN 1-55002-466-3

1. Canada — Politics and government — Humor. 2. Canadian wit and humor (English)
I. Whalley, Peter, 1921- II. Title.

FC173.N534 2003 971'.002'07 C2003-902954-9 F1008.4.N43 2003

1 2 3 4 5 06 05 04 03 02

Canadä

We acknowledge the support of the **Canada Council for the Arts** and the **Ontario Arts Council** for our publishing program. We also acknowledge the financial support of the **Government of Canada** through the **Book Publishing Industry Development Program** and **The Association for the Export of Canadian Books**, and the **Government of Ontario** through the **Ontario Book Publishers Tax Credit** program, and the **Ontario Media Development Corporation's Ontario Book Initiative.**

Care has been taken to trace the ownership of copyright material used in this book. The author and the publisher welcome any information enabling them to rectify any references or credit in subsequent editions.

J. Kirk Howard, President

Printed and bound in Canada.
Printed on recycled paper.
www.dundurn.com

Dundurn Press
8 Market Street
Suite 200
Toronto, Ontario, Canada
M5E 1M6

Dundurn Press
73 Lime Walk
Headington, Oxford,
England
OX3 7AD

Dundurn Press
2250 Military Road
Tonawanda NY
U.S.A. 14150

Contents

Introduction by Stuart McLean

Just like Peter Whalley, who drew the illustrations for this book, and has collaborated with the author on five other books over a span of almost fifty years, I have never met Eric Nicol. He calls our relationship "bloodless." It has been electronic for the most part. We talk on the telephone. But I know if I were to have tea with him, in the living room of his cottage on Saturna Island, we would have lots to talk about. And that wherever that conversation began, it would eventually come around to the subject of Canada. For much of Eric's writing, and this book is no departure, has been about this country.

"I'm patriotic," he says.

Eric is patriotic in the most Canadian of ways, his patriotism being driven by gratefulness rather than pride.

"There's certainly no other place," he says, "where I would like to live." Eric can say this with some authority. He has travelled the world, finally settling for the West — Vancouver.

"Vancouver has always been my home," he says, even though he was born in Kingston, Ontario.

The great American humorist Mark Twain wrote that humour, if is to last forever — and by forever Twain meant thirty years — must have a bit of both the preacher and teacher in it.

Eric has a bit of the preacher in him.

But as he says, "People bridle at being preached at. So, if you can sneak in through the funny bone, it's a good way."

It can be a depressing business being funny. The world, as E.B. White once wrote, may like humour, but it treats it patronizingly. "It decorates its serious artists with laurels and its wags with Brussels sprouts ... and those who take their literary selves with great seriousness are at considerable pains never to associate their name with anything funny, or flippant, or nonsensical, or light. They suspect it would hurt their reputation, and they are right."

But White knew that humour, like poetry, has an extra content. It plays close, writes White, to the big hot fire which is Truth, and sometimes the reader feels the heat.

Eric Nicol has found his way to this fire through

laughter — and he has done a better job of it than his modesty allows him to admit. He is one of a select group of Canadians who has won the Stephen Leacock Award for Humour three times. A literary hat trick.

Eric talks about his writing in an understated fashion. He says he has no "missionary zeal," that he is just trying to get a giggle. This description doesn't give the right impression of his accomplishments. In the 1940s he worked for the BBC in London, writing for a British radio sitcom. And it's worth noting that even then, even there, Eric managed to write about Canada: the show, *Leave Your Name and Number*, was about two expatriate Canadians trying to break into show business. He has published over six thousand newspaper columns. He has written several stage plays and about three dozen books.

But Eric, being Canadian, is, if nothing else, modest. He even talks about life in an off-hand manner. "I'm eighty-three, I enjoy sleeping and breathing," he says. "I also take the occasional nap."

I bet if I were lost and stumbled upon Eric's idyllic cottage in the Gulf Islands — and I had no idea who he was — it would take a long time for me to find out he is one of the most successful Canadian authors I would meet. I'll bet I would never hear that one of his plays made it to Broadway (even if it was only for one day).

On my office bookshelf, within arm's reach, I still have a book of his that I bought when I was university. I have lugged it around with me from apartment to apartment, from house to house — for *over* thirty years. Which by Mark Twain's yardstick means it has shifted from forever into the timeless ever-after. I have it still because I treasure it.

Eric Nicol is to be celebrated as a Canadian treasure. I look forward to the day we meet.

Now, on to *Canadian Politics Unplugged!*

Advisory

This is a book for people who have no idea how Canada is governed, i.e. visitors, illegal immigrants, and citizens who have lived in this country all their lives.

These folk may have a vague idea that their government involves politics, but they exercise their democratic right to remain ignorant.

This book respects that right, and indeed fortifies it.

However, political ignorance has become rampant. A recent poll found that most Canadians can't tell the political right from left. They may have a grasp on the difference between right and wrong, but fewer than half (47 percent) of those polled had the correct answer to whether the Canadian Alliance Party was to the right or left of the NDP. Granted, some members of the Canadian Alliance themselves seem unsure whether they are right wing, left wing, or the part that comes out of the coop last. But the public has the right to know.

This book attempts to distinguish the left-wing party from the right-wing, and also to show why neither wing is attached to the body politic. It boldly probes the mystery of why Canadians become aroused by politics, possibly as a substitute for a sex life. Should we view Canadian preoccupation with politics as a form of necrophilia, a nation infatuated with the walking dead rising out of Parliament Hill?

Regardless, there can be no doubt that in this country politics is a socially transmitted condition. Hence the need for a clinical study such as this to help those people who are politically active without taking the proper precautions.

As with the hazards of promiscuous sex, it is hard to have democracy without contracting politics. Safe sex is possible; safe elected representation is not. And because Canada has one of the most democratic governments on earth, it is especially prone to chronic politics that defies treatment.

Yet, though Canadians are easily aroused politically, it is not a pleasurable experience. Reason: in this country politics is not a contact sport. Canadians love and understand their ice hockey because the contest involves crushing bodychecks. Thus the smile that we trust is toothless. Unless a politician can take out his front denture for the public contest, he or she fails this criterion of serious purpose.

These and other political phenomena will be discussed, frankly and for the first time in layman's language, in the pages that follow. Among the sharp questions they will address:

Should the Fathers of Confederation have had a vasectomy?

Has the main support of Canadian unity been Wayne Gretzky's jockstrap?

Has the staid nature of the province of Ontario affected the virility of Canadian politics? (Niagara rhymes with Viagra.)

Goverament

Parliament — The Pox on Both Our Houses

The name derives from the French: *parler*. Talking. An aerobic exercise for the mouth. Also good for the knees, as members have to stand up to talk. Otherwise Parliament shows that silence is golden but talking gets a better pension.

As Pierre Trudeau demonstrated, without actually saying so, Parliament has zilch to do with government. Nothing actually gets done in the houses of Parliament. They are places where members can vocalize about something that is being done elsewhere. Possibly in the washroom.

To make sure that nothing is accomplished except talking is the job of the Speaker. Contrary to his name, the Speaker does not say anything. Unless seriously provoked. If members get carried away by emotion during an exchange of diatribes and threaten to say something significant, the Speaker bangs his gavel and cries, "Order! Order!" This wakes up the members

who have been snoozing through the discussion and gets the noisy disputants thoroughly disliked. Such open and vociferous displays of sincerity disturb the peace of Parliament and are punishable by dirty looks from both sides of the House.

In theory, Parliament is also disciplined by the sergeant-at-arms, who carries a great mace, symbolizing that what the House does really is a blow to the head. Before the House can sit, the sergeant-at-arms leads a parade into the chamber, carrying the mace that makes the members of Parliament shut up long enough for the governor general to open Parliament, close Parliament, or leave Parliament slightly ajar for the cat to get out.

The House seating follows the British model of opposing tiers of seats, with front benches reserved for party House leaders, who of course don't need to go to the bathroom as often as backbenchers.

Assembly bell

To discourage physical violence, the confronting galleries are separated by the traditional distance of two sword lengths, or one long spit.

The threat of non-verbal attack is more apparent in the House of Commons than in the Senate, where swords have been largely replaced by canes. In the Commons, members' behaviour is strongly influenced by the architecture of the Parliament buildings, which is Gothic. One definition of Gothic (*Oxford Concise*): "a style popular in the 18th-19th century novel, with supernatural or horrifying events … barbarous, uncouth." Which pretty well describes the level of debate in the Commons.

We Should Not Speak Ill of the Senate

Sometimes known as the Upper House, the Senate is no relation to Upper Canada except that both belong to history. This body corresponds roughly to Britain's House of Lords. The blood is not as blue but circulates at much the same pace, which is stately.

Senators were originally appointed for life, but it didn't work. No life appeared. Today a person remains a senator till he or she turns seventy-five, when the

The Senate

senator is wakened and quietly asked to find other sleeping accommodations.

Man proposeth, God disposeth, and the Senate reposeth.

Passing the BiLL

Canada's Senate is smaller than the House of Lords, which sleeps 1,176. Also, it has no peers, other than bladder-wise. Membership is not hereditary, and may be curable.

Instead of Lords Temporal and Lords Spiritual, the Senate has Lords Unaccountable, with their expense sheets.

Because British lords are usually better educated than Canadian senators, the level of debate is somewhat higher, and people have been known actually to listen to what is being said. This rarely happens in the Canadian Senate, but the restaurant has better coffee.

As a legislature, the Senate is part of Parliament's system of checks and balances. That is, the senator gets a check that balances his bank account. Yet he is not allowed to get near a Commons money bill. The Senate may give birth to any other kind of bill, but because of the advanced age of the parent, the bill is likely to die on the floor of the Commons. Senators pass on, rather than their bills.

The main job of the Senate, besides staying awake, is to examine a Commons bill and find that it is badly flawed but what the hell. Then everyone breaks for lunch.

The Senate's mandate is to provide "sober second thought." The "sober" part creates the most difficulty after lunch. Also, this function presumes there was first thought in the Commons, which may be more sober but doesn't act like it.

Rarely has the Senate actually blocked legislation, because any time it does so, the Commons threatens to abolish it. Abolition is a strong issue in the Senate, one on which every member is prepared to sit and be counted.

Sober second thoughts

In 1986, a Liberal senator named Hebert went on a hunger strike, in the Senate, to protest the Mulroney Government's abandonment of an activities program for troubled youth. The senator's fasting embarrassed his fellow senators because, with each day that passed without him eating or drinking in the dining room, he looked better physically than the other senators. There were pleas that he drop his starvation diet before he was in good enough shape to run for the Commons.

One criticism of the Senate is that no one should become a member of a governing body as a result of *patronage*. Patronage is the political equivalent of workmen's compensation: the prime minister compensates the recipient for having suffered a mental hernia in trying to raise funds for the party.

Recent governments have tried to reduce the number of Senate appointments by instead appointing the candidate as an ambassador abroad. If he has been a member of a rival party he may be sent to an

Speaker

embassy in a country where there is a history of embassies being burned to the ground by unruly mobs. Prime ministers have long memories.

A lesser knock against the Senate is that its members are prone to absenteeism. Senators who have been absent for less than a year are allowed back into the House without having to produce a note from their mother.

To lose his seat because of poor attendance, a senator must either die or fail to show up for two consecutive sessions of Parliament, whichever comes first. This rule is often abused, however, some senators showing up only often enough to keep their paycheques coming, not bothering to take off their coat if they have a cab waiting outside.

In the event that — because of unforeseen circumstances — a senator should find himself in the Senate, it is assumed that he will not say or do anything to draw attention to himself, let alone to national affairs. Recently Senator Pat Carney, the feisty member from the West Coast, startled the whole nation by standing up — already a bizarre act — and stating that unless Central Canada smartened up, British Columbia might beat Quebec in the race to unilateral secession. *(Vive la B.C. libre!)*

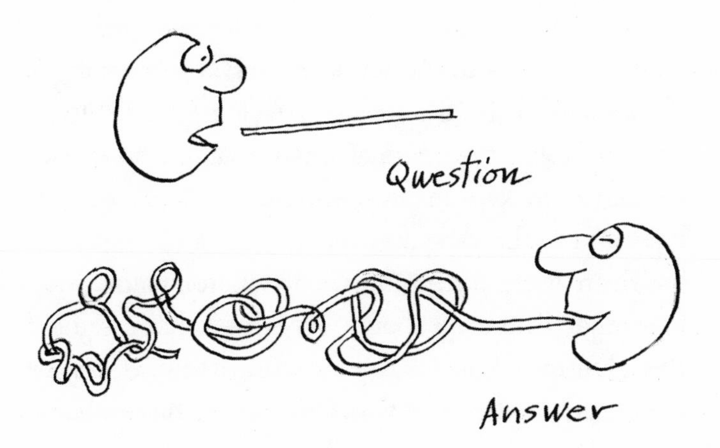

The Revolt of the Seniors

Worse, Senator Carney, a Conservative appointee, then shocked the Senate by marrying Paul White, a known Grit. This political miscegenation alone was enough to make some of the more venerable senators have a fit of the vapours.

Even more disturbing than Senator Carney has been that Britain's Labour government has assaulted the House of Lords by eliminating membership by reason of blood. While Canada's Senate has no blood to speak of, the idea of replacing political appointment with some criterion based on accomplishment appalls Ottawa. It is bad enough that people like Pat Carney are getting into the Senate despite screens on the windows without creating a *meritocracy*.

It is already tough for a politician to get into Heaven. Let him at least hope to spend eternity in the Senate.

The Commons — The Lower (Much Lower) House

The main difference between the House of Commons and the Senate is that a person must be publicly elected to get in, even if he tips the *maître d'*.

This is the house for the common people. Some are so common as to be downright vulgar. They are why the Commons has special rules about unparliamentary language. Such as *liar*, *pompous ass*, *Nazi*, *stinker*, and *mother* (when non-maternal).

MPs are constantly discovering new words that they may not use in the Commons. It is one of the main areas of exploration, now that the Arctic is pretty well mapped.

When the language gets so unprintable that the Speaker is forced to stand up and look offended, the offender has the choice of retracting the naughty word or insisting that he was misheard and that what he said merely *sounded* like a no-no. Some of the more memorable sound-alikes: "fuddle-duddle" (Pierre Trudeau's

Government
infrastructure

imperishable homonym), "some of which," "bar steward," and of course the ever-popular "Duke of Atholl."

If an MP refuses to apologize for his unparliamentary language, the Speaker may "name" him. This is serious. Especially if the member already has a name. If he objects to being named, stamps his foot, or sticks out his tongue, the sergeant-at-arms may escort him out of the chamber, banning him from the debate. Why this is considered to be a form of punishment is not clear. (Winston Churchill, noticing a fellow MP turning on his hearing aid, murmured to him: "Why do you deny yourself your natural advantage?")

In any event, ejection of a member from the Commons is a rare event because nobody was listening to him in the first place. The Speaker has no authority to eject himself. He has to keep sitting there, gamely, and exercise his judgment, which does nothing for the heart or reproductive system.

Indeed, the Speaker has such a thankless job that initially he has to be carried bodily, by the prime minister and the leader of the Opposition, to the Chair. None has gone to the Chair under the illusion that the execution will be painless. Only months or years later, when the Speaker is removed from the Chair and examined by a doctor, does he realize that he would have fared better, with lethal injection, in the Senate.

In the meantime, the Speaker has to deal with *contempt* of the Commons. The most infectious carrier of contempt for the Commons was Pierre Trudeau. Because he was a former university professor, Trudeau preferred his office as a place of work. He treated the Commons as a classroom, where he was obliged to teach an elementary course that he felt belonged in a special institution for the mentally retarded.

Trudeau responded to questions in the Commons by (a) raising his eyebrows, (b) shrugging his shoulders, or if he considered the question to be particularly idiotic, (c) both raising and shrugging, the classic Gallic reaction to the absurd.

What Trudeau never raised was his voice. Once, famously, he raised a finger, by way of response to a hostile crowd of B.C. mountain folk heckling his passage by train. But in the Commons this great statesman spoke softly and carried a big shtick.

Since Trudeau, the Commons has resumed its reputation as a daycare centre for adult children. The larger the government majority in the House — as with the recent Chrétien regimes — the less likely it is that a member will say anything worth noting. The Record reports "Some members: 'Oh! Oh!' French members: 'Oo-la-la!'"

Question period

The main role of Commons members is to show up. Their physical presence is needed for them to vote for or against a bill, as instructed. They are like Pavlov's dogs: the Assembly bell rings, and they vote, knowing that they will be rewarded with a meaty stipend. Some MPs have been trained for so long to respond with this conditioned reflex that hearing *any* bell causes them to salivate, jump up on their hind legs, and wait to be counted.

Occasionally an MP will grow restless, or ambitious, and introduce *a private member's bill.* This ilk of bill allows the members to vote according to their conscience. However, since legislation has nothing to do with conscience, avoids it like the plague, in fact, the private member's bill inevitably dies on the Order Paper. (The Order Paper is laid on the floor of the House so that the DOA bill won't make a mess.)

What will kill a bill outright is *adjournment.* Adjournment results from the Standing Order, which determines when the House is sitting. (There is no sitting order when the House is standing. But there is a standing committee that sits on privileges and decides if a member is lying. If a member *is* found to be lying, he is not allowed to sit because the House won't stand for it.)

Such committees are very important to the Commons, especially multi-partisan committees whose performance can't be blamed on anyone in particular. Committees cannot make final decisions, thus providing a model for the Commons as a whole. Only the prime minister can make a final decision, with the help of his Cabinet, his wife, his mother's ghost, and of course God when available.

When the prime minister makes a *wrong* decision, or even feels one coming on, he stays home and gives the deputy prime minister the opportunity to answer sharp questions in the House. If the PM has made a *really* bad decision he may have to leave the country entirely. Then he is on *a foreign mission*, an occurrence eventually noticed by the media.

The media are accommodated in the House by means of the press gallery. The press gallery supplements the public gallery by enabling the whole country to look down on events in the Commons, should anything happen.

The addition of TV broadcasting to the press gallery has tested the concept of broadcasting live. Televised Commons debates can remain live for only a few seconds before lapsing into a rerun of "Gilligan's Island."

The illusion of activity in the Commons is created by calling the subject of debate *the motion*. The motion usually starts in the government benches and goes 'round and 'round the House, like the "wave" in a football crowd, except that it is a slow motion and nobody is carrying the ball.

An effort to stop the motion entirely is made by Opposition members known as *the shadow cabinet.*

Shadow Cabinet

The shadow cabinet is an imaginary body composed of MPs who are Cabinet ministers in their own mind. They vigorously attack the motion that they would be making if their party were in power.

The shadow cabinet recalls Plato's famous analogy for people destitute of philosophy: prisoners in a cave who are chained so that they can see only shadows cast on the wall of the cave by a fire at the entrance, and who mistake the shadows for real people. In the Ottawa cave, the fire is put out every five years. Sometimes sooner. That rattles a few chains, but the denizens get no closer to reality.

The Power Trip (Scenic Route)

To paraphrase Lord Acton: all power craps, and absolute power craps big time.

Political power is also a steroid drug, one that proves the brain is not a muscle. It causes the politician, once elected, to lose his principles the way a girl loses her virginity: it may hurt the first time, but after that it gets easier and easier.

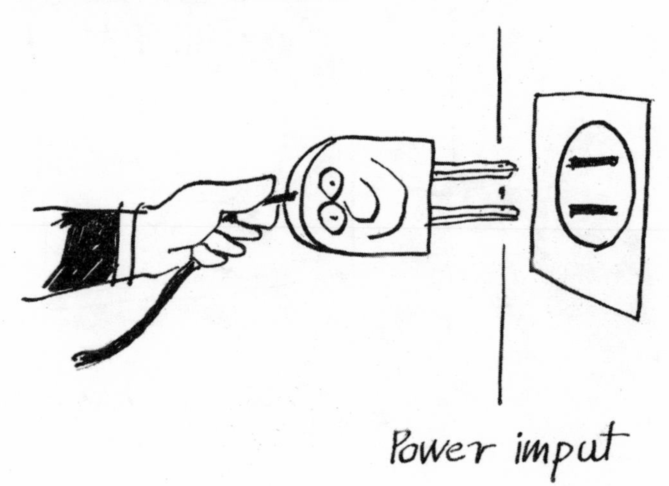

Because Canada is officially a democracy, the government must preserve the illusion that its political power is somehow related to what the people want. Or need. Or should have had before it became too late.

To accommodate this fantasy, the governing party creates *a power structure*, or leaky condo. This structure comprises a number (ever increasing) of *departments*. Which never depart. They stay right there, in the government buildings, and instead of departing they get bigger, expanding into more offices, gradually nudging other residents out of the capital. (Most of Ottawa now lives in Rockcliffe).

pick the leader

Heading the federal government power structure are a number of *ministers*, all lay. Their departments:

1. Defence
   Because Canada is the world's Number One peace-loving country — having beaten Switzerland in the finals — the main function of the minister of defence is to keep a low profile. Indeed, his profile is so low that it cannot be detected, even by radar.

Thus most Canadians are unable to name the current minister of defense. Anyone who *does* know who he is qualifies for surveillance by CSIS for possessing information not classified in the *Yellow Pages*. (CSIS is Canada's very secret service — what its initials stand for is the main secret.)

The last defence minister to make a name for himself did so because he was forced to resign after his tour of Canadian military bases in West Germany was found to have included a visit to a strip joint. Only the planes were supposed to take off. The minister was publicly chastised for inspecting the wrong facility.

2. Health and Welfare

For years Ottawa's Health Department has wrestled with the enormous problem of how to reduce cigarette smoking without damaging the fragile environment of Ontario tobacco growers' votes.

This is why Health needs to label its announcements: "Danger to health increases with amount swallowed."

As for the Welfare branch, its main responsibility is to make sure that no Canadian is too poor to buy smokes. It is also concerned about financial support of "single moms" — women who have children by means of artificial information.

3. Immigration

Canada is often described as "a country of immigrants." This annoys the hell out of the native Indians, who have been here long enough to qualify as residents.

The Immigration Department has lately had to cope with growing numbers of illegal immigrants, who are usually allowed to stay

"on humanitarian grounds." Unfortunately these grounds are not shown on any map of Canada. This is why most of the smuggled aliens stay in Canada only long enough to get fed, shaved, and manicured before slipping across the border to the U.S.

4. Finance

This minister must be a fiscal Fred Astaire, tapdancing his way through his annual budget speech to the Commons without stepping on more taxpayers' toes than absolutely necessary.

Equally important: good timing. The finance minister must be able to come up with goodies just before his party calls an election and delay the bad news of deficits till the nation's attention is distracted by some other disaster, such as Team Canada losing to Latvia.

Traditionally, the finance minister wears a red rosebud in his suit lapel on Budget Day. If, in the course of his presentation, the rose wilts visibly and all the petals fall off, it becomes a floral tribute — laid on the minister's chances of becoming the next party leader.

5. Justice

   The minister of justice is always under pressure to order the arrest of the minister of finance. Reason: the finance minister is guilty of child abuse, namely aiding and abetting the national debt that will crush the children of tomorrow. But since the justice minister is implicated by being a member of the same Cabinet gang, he concentrates on criminal activity outside Parliament Hill.

Through the Law Reform Commission, the justice minister can change the law to suit the wishes of the majority of people who are old enough to vote. Easier divorce and legal abortion are examples of what can happen to Canadians too young to mark a ballot. Even if the kid is lucky enough to make it out of the womb, he or she stands a good chance of being deprived of one parent (usually the father) and spending his or her most formative years in the bosom of the Dicky Bird Daycare.

Justice is done, like dinner.

The justice minister also provides spiritual guidance to the Human Rights Commission, which is charged with making sure that humans have rights. This helps to distinguish it from the SPCA.

6. Environment

The minister of environment, having limited authority over all matter, has pretty well discharged his duty if he drives to the office without hitting a tree.

This minister's worst enemy is environmental activists like Greenpeace that keep

reminding the world that there are other forms of life besides politicians.

The environment minister is constantly pressured by special interest groups, like hunters wanting permission to shoot anything outside city limits, logging companies that blame parks for harbouring trees, and corporations planning to build a power station whose emissions could sterilize residents within a fifty-mile radius.

The minister's response to these powerful pressures is to remain very still. Motionless. Mute as a mackerel dead of pollution. And hope to survive as an endangered species of Cabinet minister.

Above all, the environment minister must put on a happy face, even though he has lost his nose to smog.

The quality of environment is not strained, but droppeth like the acid rain from heaven.

7. Agriculture

This is the only minister who scrapes his boots before entering the House.

The agriculture minister's main job is to ensure a sustained yield of farm votes. He does this by looking and acting as rural as he can without chewing a straw and slow-spitting.

Eugene Whelan, as aggie minister — dishevelled, belly-prone, grain elevator shoes — was the one member of the Liberal Cabinet who felt safe travelling through the Prairie provinces. (Pierre Trudeau flunked the test miserably, once scolding a herd of Saskatchewan farmers for expecting him to help sell their seedy grain.)

No minister of agriculture has had the nerve to tell the grain farmers that Canada is no longer "the breadbasket of the Empire." The department is still working on a way to break the news that Queen Victoria is dead.

The international grain market has also passed away, but the government props up the body with *subsidies*. In fact subsidies have become the number one cash crop on the Canadian Prairies. A Liberal minister of agriculture developed a new strain of subsidy that is resistant to Tories. The subsidy is planted in the farmer's pocket, and four or five years later is harvested as bushels of votes for Grits.

8. Secretary of State

Contrary to popular belief, the secretary does not sit on the prime minister's lap and take dictation. He takes it standing up.

Canada's secretary of state is not as powerful as the American secretary of state, who often has breakfast with the president. The Canadian secretary of state may have breakfast with nobody but the folks at Tim Horton's.

The S of S's responsibilities include such delicate subjects as women's rights and the

Canadian Broadcasting Corporation. Any matter that demands a minimum of political intervention to allay the hostility of a significant segment of voters crosses the secretary's desk. Often without stopping.

He or she is responsible for public funding of the CBC, but treats it as a state secret. He tapes everything, but especially his mouth. Having paid for design of the CBC logo — the exploding pizza — he and the rest of the Cabinet hoped that would be the extent of programming. With imaginative use of the test pattern.

As for women's rights, the S of S lately has had to act as interlocutor for the rival demands for funds by the feminist Status of Women and the anti-feminist Real Women. This requires the judgment of Solomon, but he's not answering his pager.

In such a no-win situation, with any decision bound to alienate a large section of female voters, the normal procedure is for the secretary and other Cabinet ministers to have an exhaustive discussion behind closed, locked, and barricaded doors, then draw straws to see which minister must announce the decision to the media and be relocated by the RCMP under a different name.

9. Sports

To qualify for this post — goal post, in fact — the sports minister must be fit enough to go the extra mile, verbally.

This is an emotional ministry, because Canadians are sports fanatics, many substituting it for other organized religion. Thus the sports minister must be more discreet than in

countries where people sometimes think about something else. (Significantly, the Canadian government has no minister of sex.)

Mainly the sports minister must deal with reconciling the sponsorship of cherished athletic and sports events by breweries and tobacco companies, whose advertising is of course suspected of encouraging young Canadians to smoke and drink themselves to death — an undesirable consequence, in the view of the fussbudgets.

Thus the sports minister has to believe that he is a Jesus enhancing aquatic sport by walking on water.

10. External Affairs
    This minister is envied by other members of the Cabinet because he has an excuse for not knowing what is going on in his own country (Canada).

External Affairs also has no effect on how Canadians vote in an election, since it is always Canada's foreign policy to love *everybody*. The minister goes to UN meetings in times of crisis in order to support whoever is doing the Decent Thing. Usually it is the U.S. that is running the Decent Thing, which cues External Affairs on when to hold up the hand. And leave the room.

A winner of the Nobel Prize for Peace, Lester (Mike) Pearson was very good at External Affairs. He showed that politics should not be taken internally.

An idiot cousin of External Affairs is International Commerce, which engages in free trade negotiations with the U.S. and demonstrates that when the mouse invites the elephant to waltz, footwork is a risk factor. Else Canada gets its *sovereignty* stepped on, a small, sensitive appendage, which when national pride is aroused stands erect, though no one salutes.

In recent years International Commerce has had to contend with *globalization*. Globalization is the economic process whereby international free trade makes everything belong to Bill Gates. The head of Microsoft now controls enough wealth to be able to buy Canada if he wishes to expand the back yard of his billion-dollar home near Seattle, Washington.

11. Multiculturalism
    A real vote-getter is this minister. Must be spry enough to engage in folk dances with ethnic groups while speaking in tongues. Dresses eclectically.

The multiculturalism minister should be able to speak and write one language no better than any other, except maybe Bantu. He sees it as a compliment when people refer to the Parliament Buildings' Peace Tower of Babel. His main worry: that cornflakes boxes are getting big as crates to accommodate all the languages identifying the contents.

12. Fisheries and Oceans
This minister is badly situated (in Ottawa) to be conscious of what is happening in Canada's fisheries and oceans. He may have a basic

understanding of the connection between fish and water, but beyond that he must depend on reports of fisheries officers who visit the country's coasts and look into the parts that are wet enough to support marine life.

The minister may of course go fishing in the Ottawa River, but catching discarded condoms is no substitute for first-hand experience with the plight of the Newfie cod industry.

This minister's main accomplishment in recent years has been to automate the coastal lighthouses to save money, rather than lives. Sailors and cruise passengers rarely vote in a Canadian federal election, so Fisheries and Oceans emphasizes the importance of swimming lessons in its modernizing of the country's beacons.

13. Intergovernmental Affairs

This is the most multisyllabic minister in the Cabinet. No one covets the position because the politician has to remain totally sober just to give his job description. *Spelling* the damn thing is out of the question.

So, assuming that the intergovernmental minister has qualified with higher education

and a flair for tongue twisters, what does he *do*? Well, his main job is to say "No." Or, alternatively, "Non." This is his reply to the provincial premiers who meet regularly in order to synchronize their demands for more federal financing. They know in advance what his response will be ("No" or "Non"), but their failure to demand more money would make the intergovernmental affairs minister redundant. There is a certain courtesy among Canadian politicians to respect one another's jobs while making the public outcry that validates their own. As ballet, it is as ritualized as anything produced by Japan's kabuki theatre.

These are but a sampling of federal Cabinet ministers. There are many more. Multiplying like mice. The group photo has now become impossible, even with a wide lens, unless the shot is taken from space.

Original number of Cabinet ministers: twelve. By Mulroney's time: forty. Today, it's anybody's guess, if able to count over a hundred.

To try to co-ordinate the activities of this horde is the job of the Privy Council. Which meets in the john because there can be only so many seats.

All of these Cabinet ministers, councils, and their committees defer to an individual appropriately called the *prime minister*.

The Prime Minister

This is the only federal minister considered to be important enough to be given a chauffeur. He also doesn't need to be smart enough to pass the driver's test.

If times are good, the prime minister gets the chauffeur *and* a car. His transportation is assured till the next election or the gas tank shows empty, whichever comes first

The duties of the prime minister are not clear, and he works very hard to keep it that way.

The part of the indescribable job that the prime minister enjoys most is *attending conferences*, where he is photographed with other heads of state who need to get out of town. In these photo ops he gets to stand beside the shorter heads of major states. This is why the Canadian prime minister really needs to be a tall person who stands out in a crowd. Japan's prime minister can afford to be short because his country is pretty dinky too, even though it does make better cars.

Canada, being vast geographically, must be represented photographically by a six-footer or better. Joe Clark was doomed from the outset. Mackenzie King got away with being dumpy by posing for all photos sitting at his desk. King may have stood up at some point in his career, but never in company before a camera.

The PM resigns

These conferences include:

The Commonwealth Conference. Oddly named, since wealth is one thing the conferees don't have in common. What they *do* have in common is the Crown. They share the Queen. Or, if she is busy buying a new hat, they get a prince. So one way or another the Commonwealth Conference gets a shot of royalty, a tested deodorant. Also the Canadian prime minister gets to be photographed standing beside the head of India or Ghana, who is usually shorter, though a snappier dresser.

The Economic (Big Seven, Big Nine, or more) Conference. This occasion enables Canada's PM to have his picture taken with a wholly different lineup of stately heads, including the president of the United States.

The Peace Mission. Prime Minister Trudeau was very good at this method of avoiding Mrs. Trudeau. Typically the PM visits a number of foreign capitals and tells the media that peace is the best way to avoid war. Thanks to peace missions the world recognizes Canada to be a dove (if not a sitting duck) rather than a hawk.

Where Canada's prime ministers come up short is not in height but in *persona*. Pierre, obviously, was endowed with a personality. But he was an aberration, a freak even. Indeed he almost overdid it. Many Canadians — especially women — actually saw him as *charming*. His Tory opponents viewed this as an abuse of office, if not actual treason. Even some Liberals felt more comfortable when the leadership fell to Jean Chrétien, whose personality was charm-free.

In contrast, American presidents work harder at appearing human. Jimmy Carter ate peanuts in public. Nixon went on TV with his dog, as well as his wife. Reagan chopped wood at his ranch, in full view of the cameras. And Bill Clinton had illicit sex *right in the White House*, something that female interns in the House of Commons can only hallucinate about. And while some PMs have exposed themselves on the golf course, none has looked as lovable as Ike flailing in a sand trap.

As a person, the only thing the prime minister has going for him is that people feel sorry for him, being stuck in Ottawa for days at a time. For him to be interesting as well may be an unreasonable demand.

The Cabinet

When all these ministers are brought together, in a properly ventilated room, they become *the Cabinet.* We usually think of a cabinet as a storage place where we keep things we don't need. The definition holds.

The prime minister meets with the other Cabinet members from time to time to find out if any of them has done anything, or plans to do something. It is usually a short meeting.

It is harder for a gay minister to get into the Cabinet if he has come out of the closet.

All Cabinet ministers are constantly jockeying for position to replace the prime minister, should he become the victim of fair play. But it is considered to be bad form if the aspirant appears too eager. Hanging around the PM's house, for instance. Or chatting up his chauffeur.

Anticipating the junking of the government Cabinet, the main party in opposition casts what is

called a "shadow cabinet." This umbrageous body consists of MPs who follow the existing Cabinet ministers around — to the washroom, for instance — hoping to catch them doing something naughty. Some opposition MPs have been in the shadow for so many years that they have developed moss and eventually have to be power-washed out of the legislature.

The Monarchy

At the very top of Canada's political totem pole is the British monarch. Lately a queen — Elizabeth Two — who reigns but does not rule, much like an NHL referee during Stanley Cup playoffs.

For day-to-day reigning over Canada the monarch depends on *the governor general*, a Canadian personage with a natural talent for pomp and circumstance and no criminal record. The governor general is housed in Ottawa but has to keep smiling, because that is her main public function.

Her other job is to open Parliament. Parliament can't open without her. She has the key. Where she keeps it is a state secret, because there are a lot of people out there who believe that opening Parliament is like opening Pandora's box: nothing but trouble comes out of it.

All of which ritual costs the taxpayers money and raises the well-worn question: Should the monarchy

The Monarchy

be abandoned? The option to become a de-royaled republic is one of many political matters about which Canadians have no strong feelings.

Others point out the republican expense of having to change the name of such things as the Royal Canadian Mounted Police, Crown counsel, and D.G. Regina on the loonie. Also, de-monarched, Canada would need to have some other person to be head of state. A president, like France and the U.S.A.? A post associated with hanky-panky, sexual and/or political trespasses unthinkable in the Queen's rep? Not likely, till the governor general is caught in bed with the leader of the Opposition. Even then Newfoundland would balk at dumping the monarchy, because London feels closer than Ottawa.

Canadian republicanism is caught between the Rock and a hard place.

The Parties

Canadians are party animals. When two Canadians get together, they have a beer. When three get together, they form a political party.

In Canada, as in the mother country, the two traditional political parties are the Conservatives and the Liberals. The main advantage of being a Liberal is never having to say you're Tory.

Traditionally, the Conservative Party has become associated with representing the interests of the rich and privileged, and acting as though Charles Dickens had written nothing but a note for the milkman. So, to try to correct the image of an obese, top-hatted, frock-coated toff wearing spats, the Canadian party changed its name to *Progressive* Conservative. And threw away the cigar. Or at least didn't smoke in public.

But blue has remained the PC racing colour. The party is loyal to blue because blue could never be confused with red, which is of course the colour

Provincial-Federal negotiations

of Communism. The Liberals are red, but it's a sort of light red. Not pink, of course. That's socialist. It's rosy red. Critics say that Liberal red is the shade of the ink the party puddles with its spending policies.

Especially as federal government. In recent years Ottawa has given the country a steady diet of Grits, causing the people to have an abnormal movement (the Canadian Alliance Party).

The Canadian Alliance party was a wedding of the Reform Party with a party to be named later. The Reform Party remained as a splinter group of conservatives who sought to introduce integrity into federal politics. The tendency of Canadian Tories to splinter readily is a symptom of the political timber grown in Western Canada.

Thus it was Alberta's Preston Manning who, as leader of the Reform Party, carried high principles to the House of Commons, only to be required to leave them at the door.

A curious phenomenon of Canadian politics is that more new, moralistic parties are generated in the Prairie provinces than in parts of the country where decency is kept under control.

Usually the founder of the new party is a former church minister who has failed to recognize that politics is the art of the possible, not the will of God. He believes that with help of the Supreme Being (his wife) he can make an honest woman of that old whore on Parliament Hill.

The dream is usually short-lived.

One such party was Social Credit, which like the Reform Party had its genesis in Canada's political holy land. Alberta's Social Credit, whose high priest was William Aberhart, actually spread into British Columbia — something like a messiah taking the message into downtown Sodom and Gomorrah.

The early Socreds were in fact evangelists who believed that the path to financial prosperity lay in giving the people money to spend on good works. This was a switch on the money changers in the temple as originally formatted. "Funny money," as it was blasphemously termed by political naysayers, took the form of the Prosperity Certificate, which entitled the holder to a share in Good Times. Because in this period the country was in the grips of the Great Depression, Social Credit had the appeal of Communism but with more sanctified bookkeeping.

The people adored Social Credit. It had made Mammon a respectable suburb of Edmonton. Even after the faith got chilled in its birthplace, Social Credit survived for decades in parts of the country with a weaker grasp on reality. In B.C. it flourished under the premiership of W.C. ("Wacky") Bennett. This was the blessed ministry of the Father and the Son (William "Bill" Bennett). Under their divine guidance, the province never looked back — a mistake, as it was being overtaken by the forces of fiscal evil: New Democrats.

The New Democratic Party, or Endeepee, began as a leftish cult called the Co-operative Commonwealth Federation, which soon became the CCF because nobody could remember what the initials stood for.

The party's first leader, Tommy Douglas, is recognized to be the father of socialized medicine. What is socialized medicine? Socialized medicine means that a patient gets to meet a lot more people in the doctor's waiting room.

Douglas gained power as leader of the first socialist government in Canada, mostly because he had a good sense of humour. The farmers of Saskatchewan were busy starving at the time, suffering from deep depression (1930–2002), and were glad to vote for anyone who could give them a chuckle.

socialized medicine

After the amusing CCF changed its initials to NDP it expanded to Ottawa, where it wasn't nearly as funny as when it became the Government of British Columbia, where it became hysterical.

A much more serious party is Quebec's Parti Québécois, which is hardly ever good for a giggle. The reason: its agenda consists mostly of separating Quebec from the rest of Canada, a major operation that could involve some bleeding. Especially painful would be the loss of the Canadian dollar. Transfer payments from Ottawa would be amputated, putting a lot of strain on circulation of the Quebec franc. And it is probably too late to hope for a transfusion from Louis XV.

Finally, Canada has a smattering of fringe — one might say lunatic fringe — parties. Because of an oversight in the Canadian legal system, there is no law against forming a political party. Often it happens in a private home, in a respectable neighbourhood. A couple of consenting adults get together, have a few drinks, indulge in political intercourse and — bingo! — another party is born. Dependent on public welfare. Like:

1. The Unity Party. This party consists entirely of people who are sick of all the other parties. Its aim: to take the politics out of government. Motto: don't get mad, get even crazier.

2. The Marijuana Party. Not, as one might assume, the party party. This party just wants to legalize marijuana, which is already a major cash crop in British Columbia. The plan is to replant B.C.'s vast deforested areas with cannabis, so the German tourists will just have to inhale to get turned on by the province's scenery. Motto: let him who is without sin get stoned.

3. The Feng Shui Party. Favoured by a sector of the West Coast's large Chinese population,

the Feng Shui credo is that having politicians standing behind their promises is bad luck. Replace them with chop suey joints.

Choosing the Party Leader

If the camel is a horse designed by a committee, the jackass is a party leader chosen by *a leadership convention.*

The leadership convention involves the only kind of Canadian election that includes a display of emotion. Needless to say, it's overdone. Normally the dour persons whom the world recognizes as the essence of the national phlegm suddenly go berserk. They put on funny campaign hats and parade around the convention centre jigging banners and shouting themselves hoarse. All to elect as a party leader someone who, if rational, none would trust to borrow his garden shears.

E pluribus hokum.

One ballot doesn't satisfy the delegates to a party convention. No way. They have to have a whole series of ballots, each ballot taking longer than the previous ballot, a veritable orgy of balloting. It is the political version of the multiple orgasm.

Nomination speech

On the first ballot the delegates vote to eliminate the candidate who has made the mistake of:

(a) saying something that had substance, or
(b) skimping on his campaign potato chips, or
(c) having a name like Howard Zilch — last on the ballot list.

On the second ballot, the delegates whose candidate lost on the first ballot vote for the candidate who will lose on the third ballot. The fourth ballot is declared invalid because one of the scrutineers has died of old age. Only on the fifth (or more) ballot is the winner declared: the man or woman least likely to do anything to offend anybody.

In Roman times this method of choosing a leader was known as the *reductio ad absurdum*, or sorting down to the silly. It was the system that made Nero look good, comparatively.

Today, creationists cite the political leadership convention as proof that Darwin was wrong in postulating the survival of the fittest. Natural selection,

Electioneering

they point out, plays no role in the convention hall. Instead, control of the party herd is gained largely by:

(a) the candidate's *nomination acceptance speech.* This dramatic monologue has to be emotional enough to assure the delegates that he/she can get wound up without a key.

She/he must convince them that he/she has her/his finger on the pulse of the nation/province/city/condo, his/her ear to the ground, her/his shoulder to the wheel, a fire in his/her belly and the stamina to endure the choreographed standing ovation.

Having great legs also helps, though less so for the male candidate.

(b) the candidate's *party favours.* These are not just the convention balloons. After a leadership candidate has been dropped from contention and has had a good cry, representatives of candidates still in the running approach him — cautiously — with a deal for his transfer of support to one of the survivors. What the surviving candidate offers in exchange depends on how badly he needs the extra votes. If it's only a few, he may just offer

#1

The Leader

the loser a ride home. But if he requires a lot more votes to stand a chance on the next ballot he may offer the eliminated candidate:

(i) a Cabinet post, or
(ii) a year's free laundry service, or
(iii) Chilliwack, B.C.

This ritual gives the winning leadership candidate early training in corruption, if not already unchaste. Even before he gains power he has made himself beholden to an untold number of people who expect recompense earlier than being remembered in his will.

In this regard, President George W. Bush is said to owe his successful candidacy almost entirely to his uncanny ability to remember the name of every person he has ever met. Bush's brain is a living registry of voters' names. His mind has room for little else. Dubya has depended on his staff of advisers — all of whose names he recalls instantly — to attend to other matters of state, whether national or international. It is enough that he can shake hands and rattle off a name simultaneously, without prompting.

Bush's gift, and the ultimate glory it has won him as the politician's politician, should serve as both warning and inspiration to the Canadian would-be politician who has difficulty putting a name to any face but his own.

Also a liability: a clammy handshake. Short of wearing gloves on all occasions, including state dinners, nothing can be done about the wimpy, pasty paw clasp.

Other personal qualities (if any): Occasionally a party leader is chosen because he has a personality. Sometimes described as *charisma*. The first, and possibly last, Canadian party leader to display real charisma was Pierre Trudeau. He did it by diving into swimming pools, skiing down steep slopes, and dating pretty women who showed everything but an interest in politics.

Pierre could look intelligent on TV without the help of special lighting. The twinkle in his eye indicated a mind at work without a court order.

Pierre captivated his Liberal leadership convention by demonstrating his total disdain for politics. Nothing charms a Canadian electorate more than convincing evidence that the political process is beneath contempt. Thus Trudeau gratified a national inferiority complex by not only *pretending* to resist being drafted by the leadership convention but by showing the unmistakable demurral of a man who is being dragged into a brothel that has an inferior wine list.

Axiom: *Anyone who appears eager to run this country is exhibiting the first symptoms of mental and/or moral decline.*

Thus Trudeau fought off pride of office. Instead of blandishing the people from his campaign train, he gave them The Finger *en passant* Revelstoke, B.C.

His was single-digit contempt for political protocol.

Voters temporarily abandoned Pierre for Joe Clark. But Clark had so much obvious respect for the political process that he lasted only a few months before the restoration of Pierre the Indifferent.

In Canadian politics, half aloof is better than none.

Having watched Brian Mulroney's hair turn grey in a matter of weeks after being elected prime minister, every Canadian knows that it takes a very special kind of person to seek the nomination as party leader: a masochist. One who realizes that he will be pilloried in the press, disfigured by cartoonists, and eviscerated by editorial writers. The public must therefore suspect that this person let himself become party leader to supplement his sleeping on a bed of spikes.

Often the party leadership candidate is a self-made millionaire who wants to give something back to the country. If he just returned the money, there would be no trouble. But, alas, once a man or woman *becomes* imbued with the lust for public service, he or she will stop at nothing till the public has been served. Roasted. On a platter with an apple in its mouth.

This exalted mission doesn't get compromised till

the winning candidate makes his *victory speech.* Then he is suddenly joined on the platform by all his relatives. They stand behind and beside him, beaming, some visibly drooling at the prospect of enhanced income and monogrammed underwear.

Finally, after expressing his humbleness in the moment of victory, the chosen candidate declares that he will win the election, with God's help — and his wife takes a bow.

The Election — How Everyone Gets to Share the Blame

Every country gets the kind of government it deserves, but being an electoral democracy rubs it in. In Canada, a person can escape responsibility for an election only by being:

1. under eighteen,
2. an illegal immigrant, or
3. on leave of absence from his or her right mind.

Nobody returns to Canada just to vote in an election, but Canadians have been known to *leave* the country to escape an election. For this reason advance polls are held, making it almost impossible for an adult Canadian to avoid complicity in the outcome of an election.

It is no coincidence that the age for voting in an election is the same as for buying liquor. Both are rites of adulthood that nobody is proud of.

Pre-election Testing

To make electoral matters worse, each registered voter is allowed to vote only once. The good old days are gone, when a truly conscientious person could vote several times in exchange for future considerations. Which he drank later.

The only reward for trudging to the polling place — often in foul weather — is to have discharged a duty. (Attempts to introduce a duty-free polling station, with liquor sold at attractive prices, have long since been abandoned in Canada. Instead, election day has the atmosphere of a national day of mourning. Authorities no longer close the pubs for the day, but relatively few voters take advantage of the excuse that they were drunk at the time.)

Result: voters stare at the ballot's list of candidates as if checking the dinner menu on the *Titanic*.

Elections were more congenial in the U.S.S.R. because voters had only one party to vote for. The Communist Party. This relieved them of the agony of choosing. Or later displaying a bumper sticker: DON'T BLAME ME — I VOTED FOR TROTSKY.

Nor is a Canadian election enlivened, as in some emerging democracies, by the threat of mob violence. If the Canadian voter, going to the polling station in his neighbourhood school, sees a grim figure standing at the entrance holding a rifle, he can safely assume that it is just one of the teachers.

And Canadian students are not seen rioting in the streets, unless the election happens to coincide with high school grad night.

To aggravate the dispirited tone of a Canadian federal election, the country's five time zones mean that people on the West Coast are still voting after people on the East Coast have elected the next government. This creates the situation in which Newfoundlanders are the first to know what has happened — an intolerable perversion of the normal. British Columbia, in particular, feels like the last to reach the scene of a disaster.

Another reason federal elections are less resented in the States: Americans have the satisfaction of voting more or less directly for the person they want to be president, unless his name is Dubya. But Canadians can vote only *indirectly* for the prime minister, by voting for the party candidate in their riding, a person they may have identified as a certified idiot.

The voter may then see his candidate elected, but the party go down to defeat, leaving him with double reason to join a religious cult that believes the voting booth to be the devil's outhouse — in which anyone who makes the sign of the cross on the ballot is doomed to spend an eternity of filling out government forms.

Yet another reason American elections contribute less to alcoholism than do the Canadian: they are held at appointed intervals. Every four years. Americans know *well in advance* exactly what day in November they will be able to get rid of a president and at least half the Congress. It is part of their Thanksgiving. Such regularity, not dependent on eating fibrous food, adds greatly to the stability of American politics and lets the people get pretty wild in other areas of public life.

In contrast, Canadian elections are held at the whim of the prime minister or premier. The outer

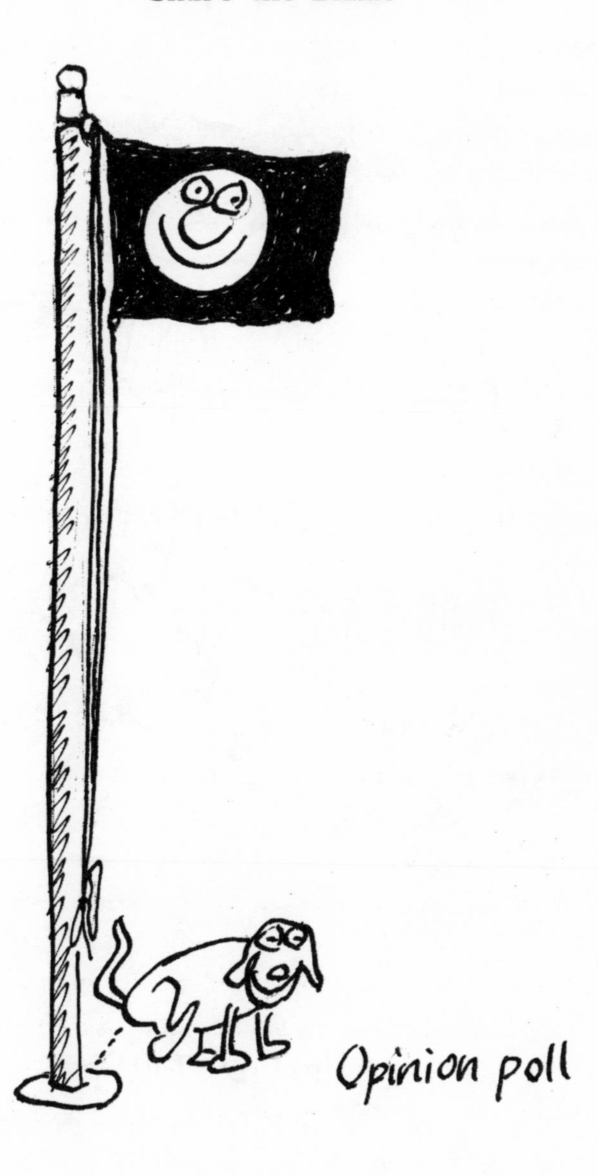
Opinion poll

The Civil Service

limit of endurance may be five years, but the term will seem longer to the people waiting for the writ — like the other shoe — to be dropped.

(Note: no one has ever seen this fateful writ. All we know about it is that being dropped is its sole function.)

The government waits till the last opportune moment to drop this writ: when the wind is right, the planets are aligned, and the tea leaves are propitious. Also essential is that the election not conflict with the Stanley Cup playoffs. Dropping the puck outranks dropping the writ.

Provincial Politics — A Regional Disturbance

In Britain, the word *province* is commonly applied to parts of the country where theatrical productions occur because they are not ready for London's West End. In Canada, however, the stage shows are called *provincial legislatures*. And the provinces have actual names. Ten of them. Several of these provinces are large enough to think of themselves as separate countries, if not planets.

Meantime, much of Ottawa's governing of Canada consists of tossing bags of peanuts to ten restless elephants and three muskoxen, whose premiers meet regularly for a first-ministers' conference invariably described as "productive." What they produce is another first-ministers' conference. Held someplace else. (This is the only thing that the first ministers are able to reach agreement on: where to hold the next conference. They can then go home feeling good about themselves and the state of the country's unity of purpose.)

Provincial politics provide more variety and comedy than the federal productions. They have more parties. None of them are stag parties, but sometimes the police do have to be called. [See *Parties*.]

The only province staid enough to have only two main parties — the Conservatives and the Liberals — is Ontario, which regards all the other provinces to be certifiable.

The provinces to the west of Ontario have served up a dog's breakfast of Grits, Tories, NDP, Alliance, Socreds, Green, Marijuana, and Rhinoceros (blowing their own horn). No one should enter this political jungle without a guide.

Provincial politics

In British Columbia the provincial Liberal and Conservative parties — both only distantly related to their federal namesakes — at one time almost faced extinction as the result of unnatural intercourse called "coalition." (Coalition is the worst thing that can happen when two parties get together without taking the proper precautions. Not only is it not curable but jumping into bed with another party is hard to explain to the children.)

The B.C. coalition of Liberals and Conservatives happened while both parties were under the influence of the New Democratic Party. But the coalition served only to drive some conventional politicians into the Social Credit Party, which had no relations with any other party except God.

The Parties God Forgot

Social Credit had its nativity scene in Alberta, where finding Jesus had been largely replaced by finding oil. Alberta is the only province in which the Conservatives have been seen as left wing. The Western Separatist Party has had some considerable support there, but is tainted by association with the B.C. branch, which is anarchist when driving in snow.

Central Alberta also supports a number of Aryan Nation parties that aim to change the name of Red Deer to White Deer and have the tar sands segregated into blacks and coloureds.

Saskatchewan became the birthplace of the Canadian Commonwealth Federation Party, the party with the most syllables ever produced by a Prairie province. The CCF leaned to the left because Saskatchewan was in poor shape: a plain rectangle with no redeeming features. At that time (the thirties) its economy depended on farmers in the Ukraine having a bad harvest. The success of the CCF was closely tied to an abundance of Russian grasshoppers.

Manitoba, "The Friendly Province," seems to tolerate all political parties well, unless the party advocates overthrow of the Blue Bombers. Confrontational politics is avoided because there is already enough hot air blowing down Portage Avenue.

Manitoba is also called "The Keystone Province," because if it weren't there in the middle all the other provinces would topple into anarchy.

Manitobans are also content to be politically boring because they can rest on the laurels of having produced the most exciting politician in the country's history: Louis Riel. What made Riel especially

memorable in Canada's politics was that he was at various times (a) declared insane, (b) elected to Parliament, and (c) hanged for murder.

This versatility has only recently been recognized as an exemplary performance. It has given Manitoba some of the charisma of a banana republic, without the dependence on marketing illegal drugs.

Also, there is a growing belief that Riel truly was divinely inspired in founding the province and that Brandon should be renamed St. Louis.

Comparatively dull, in adjoining Riel's spirited fields of battle, Ontario produces Conservative governments slightly to the right of Ivan the Terrible. To Ontarians the Liberals represent something dangerously akin to Marxist-Leninists. They are comfortable only when the province is geared to the Big Blue Machine, a Tory apparatus whose function is to keep things running exactly as they are.

Politically, Ontario is the spiritual home of the status quo. The province is so wealthy that everyone thinks that change is something left to tip the waiter.

It was as a symbol of Ontario's political superiority that Toronto built the CN Tower, Canada's highest structure, representing the stature to look down on

Western Rielism

parts of the country where buildings are merely accommodation.

Ontario is mildly discomfited by proximity to Quebec. Quebec has sort of ruined the neighbourhood. The fact that the French were there first only makes it harder for Ontario to dissociate itself from the volatile politics next door.

Accustomed to quiet, respectable, pipe-smoking premiers, Ontario has been shocked by Quebec leaders like René Lévesque who drop cigarette ash all over the Queen's domain.

Quebec politics are unique in that the province considers itself to be a sovereign state whose monarch is still Louis the Umpteenth. Louis is dead, by most accounts, but to the Québécois he is still more lively than Elizabeth the Whatever.

They call their provincial legislature "*L'Assemblé Nationale*." The National Assembly. Because Quebec is a nation in its own mind. As such it is in addition to Canada's First Nations, or Indians. Canada is a country rich in nations, more so than the United States, which has to struggle along with only one nation. Indivisible. One wonders how they manage.

Quebec nationalism, like Scotland's nationalism, is fuelled by a consciousness of economic and cultural oppression, but flavoured with garlic rather than

Gaelic. In recent years the ruling Parti Québécois has fanned the sense of francophonic identity, preserving the sanctity of the French language by dictating that cereal boxes be totally bilingual, regardless of the collateral damage to Snap, Crackle, and Pop.

Finally, completing the crazy quilt of Canada's provincial politics, we have the Maritime provinces, which don't seem to be too fussy about what party is in power, so long as the premier is not caught trying to have sex with a lobster.

As all of the Maritime provinces have a high rate of unemployment, their MLAs concentrate on programs that will get them re-elected. Result: there is almost no turnover in East Coast politicians.

So, what *do* these ten provinces and the politically nondescript territories have in common? They all have a *lieutenant-governor*. As the sovereign's representative, the lieutenant-governor opens each legislative session, then leaves the building before he or she can be blamed for what happens in it.

The LG's main job — which he or she does sitting down to avoid motion sickness — is to read what is called *the speech from the throne*. Because the speech was actually written by the premier, the reading is a sort of ventriloquist act, though rarely as funny as Kermit the Frog.

The speech outlines what the government proposes to do unless cooler heads prevail. In return for mouthing this litany of pipe dreams, the lieutenant-governor gets to live in a quite nice place, furnished with genuine flunkies, until he or she retires or develops a terminal stutter.

Besides the job of lieutenant-governor, all the provinces share a strong desire to get as much money from the federal government as they can without actually holding up a local branch of the Bank of Canada. These gratuities are known as *equalization payments*. Under the Constitution, all provinces are born equal but some squawk louder than others.

Ottawa tries to hush these financially incontinent provinces by sticking a fiscal pacifier in their budget. It is never enough. The provinces are constantly rattling their crib, bawling for more money from the feds. It is one of Canada's more enduring domestic scenes, right up there with *Anne of Green Gables*.

The Oracle of Media

Like the word *politics*, *media* doesn't know whether it is singular or plural. To the press, the word is, naturally, singular. In unity there is strength, if not respect.

But what, exactly, does *media* collectivize? Newspapers, obviously. Some radio and TV. Magazines? The Internet? Aunt Fanny, who broadcasts news for her entire neighbourhood?

Because of this ill-defined constituency, *The Oxford Concise Dictionary* tut-tuts quietly at the concept of one media: "pl. of MEDIUM. Use as a mass noun with a singular verb is common (e.g. *the media is on our side*) but is generally disfavoured (cf. AGENDA, DATA)."

Disfavoured or not, *media* as a single voice suits political parties better than the connotation that not all members of the choir are on the same page. Evidence of a variety of views among the public complicates the task of a party spin doctor. He has to

The Pundit

operate on people who are awake, and complications can set in.

Yet the media do have considerable influence on Canadian politics. Indeed they provide life support for some political events, such as federal and provincial elections, which are otherwise one of the country's main sources of apathy. For instance they provide a forum for that election-time phenomenon: *the political pundit*. The pundit is usually a university professor of political science who, like the groundhog on his day, emerges from his office every four years to predict something. Unfortunately, politics is an inexact science, right up there with phrenology and palmistry. To little avail, therefore, is the attempt by the media's pundit to make political analysis look more rational than something Macbeth's witches might come up with.

Because most of the major media — newspapers and TV — are privately owned, their natural political inclination is to the right, while appearing to be vertical. As with the Leaning Tower of Pisa, it is a constant challenge for these media to be less than upright without overdoing it.

Rarely do the lead editorials in mighty organs like *National Post*, *The Globe and Mail*, and *The Montreal Gazette* promote the cause of a socialist party like the NDP. While not as paranoid as the media in the U.S.,

C.B.C.

where even the word *liberal*, when applied to politics, causes a shudder and peed pants, Central Canada's media owners are modest enough to turn out the lights before jumping into bed with Big Business.

The main media exception, politically, is the Canadian Broadcasting Corporation, publicly owned and therefore freer to suggest that the Emperor has no clothes — or at least is down to his skivvies.

The CBC is a grey eminence that turns pink in certain lights.

The Opinion Poll

"How do I know what I think till I hear what I say?" This source of personal opinion is inadequate for people, like Canadians, who are relatively taciturn unless supported by a bar stool. And they may not remember what they voiced as their firm opinion once they've sobered up.

Thus they may become influenced by *the opinion poll* in contributing to the outcome of a political election. Like the lemmings — which also inhabit a northern zone — our people prefer to be part of a majority trend, albeit one heading over a cliff.

No one wants to be identified as a loner in politics. ("That's Weird Willie. He voted for a candidate that the polls said had no chance of winning. Let's yank his chain!")

This does not mean that Canadians don't have strong, individual opinions about things other than politics. Beer, for instance. We don't check with an

investigating reporting

opinion poll before choosing our ale. We trust TV beer commercials. But we put no credence in the paid political announcement.

This skepticism has made the fortunes of Mr. Gallup and Mr. Reid, whose public opinion polls intimidate people's judgment with highly volatile percentages, said to be accurate within five percent of a wild guess.

These opinion polls are especially tyrannous in Canada, where nobody has a fixed view about politics except that they are hazardous to mental health and may in fact be a factor in the incidence of erectile dysfunction in men and false labour for women.

Opinion polls are less virulent in the United States, where people are usually either Democrats or resolute Republicans. For life. They may divorce their wife or husband, but political party allegiance is handed down from generation to generation, like a grandfather clock. The American who defies family tradition by jumping from the Grand Old Party elephant to the Demodonkey, or from the ass to the pachyderm, becomes a black sheep.

Coalition

But Canadians, politically, are not lifelong anything. They can change parties as readily as they change their underwear. And usually for the same reason: something is starting to smell.

At any given moment a Canadian — the *same* Canadian — may be a Liberal federally, a Conservative provincially, a Green municipally, and an anarchist domestically. Or (most likely) an Undecided. Every election poll shows the Undecideds to be doing quite well, and the subsequent low turnout of voters proves that the Undecideds have in fact won. They are the only group of registered voters who, after an election, can fairly say, "Don't blame *me* — I didn't vote for *any* of the bastards."

Separation

Would Canada's provinces be more interesting politically if they had a legal separation? For instance, would it liven things up for everybody if Quebec separated from the main, so to speak, body?

Many Quebeckers seem to think so. The only value they see in the present relationship is that they get to use the Canadian dollar (*le dollar*). Separated, Quebec would have to create its own currency. Find some substitute for the image of the Queen on the coins and bills. Whom could Quebeckers agree on? Celine Dion? Rocket Richard? The peerless Lily St. Cyr, who separated herself from everything but her high heels?

However, these are details. No question, independence movements are very chic in the new millennium. Even Scotland, which the world has seen as quite content to be just a scraggy area surrounding Nessie and the Queen's Balmoral Castle, has got its kilt in a twist. To say nothing of separatists in Spain, the Balkans, the Middle East, Africa, South America, and West Vancouver.

In this severance race, Quebec's movement to separate from TROC (The Rest of Canada) is the senior revolt. Western Canada has to take a number. Some Canadian *Anglais* — commonly known to Quebeckers as *les maudits Anglais*, or mouldy English — would say that French Canadians have been revolting from day one.

The federal government has long tried to appease Quebec, letting it fly its own national flag — a lily that looks like the maple leaf only to the botanically confused — and tolerating the Quebec language law requiring shop signs to have the French words larger than the English. As in MCDONALD'S/McDonald's.

These concessions have not allayed the fear of many Quebeckers that their French culture will be overcome by the sheer weight of Anglicisms like "cheeseburger" and "hooters."

To try to gauge the degree of enthusiasm for separation in Quebec, the federal government held a *referendum* — something to be handled with kid gloves. Often the mere *threat* of a referendum is enough to make people lose interest in an issue, and possibly in sex. It is a depressant. People sense that the referendum may oblige them to think about whatever the vital question is and to make a choice that could put them in a minority group, along with foot fetishists.

But this did not deter the federal government from holding the famous 1995 Quebec Referendum on sovereignty, a dramatic event that, as expected, decided nothing. It did, however, stir up a certain amount of emotion, something not easy to do outside a hockey rink. There was even some talk that a Quebec referendum should be held as an annual event, like Halloween, but for adults only.

The Parti Québécois has said that another referendum on sovereignty is number one on its agenda. Number two on the agenda is to wait till there is a

Bilingualism byplay

guarantee that the Yes (Oui) vote will outnumber the No (Non) vote.

Establishing when this might occur may require a special referendum. No government wants to spend millions just to learn something it doesn't want to know. It will wait till referenda are on special. With at least a one-year warranty.

The Canadian Civil War

The Americans had one, and Canadians nearly always have what the Yanks have had, only later.

So far, a Canadian civil war has been unthinkable. For one thing, it couldn't be a war between the North and the South. Canadian politics are not built that way. It would have to be a civil war between the East and the West. Competing with the Grey Cup game.

However, the two parts of Canada most likely to become violent in order to get separated from Ottawa are (in order of seniority): (1) Quebec, and (2) the Western provinces — B.C., Alberta, and (depending on the crop year) Saskatchewan. The Maritimes are another possibly revolting region, but they will have to take a number.

A Quebec versus Canada civil war would be the most devastating because so many Ottawa MPs depend on being able to slip away to Montreal for R & R after doing sweet nothing.

Can-Que face-off

Scenario: hostilities break out after failure to negotiate an agreement on who owns the St. Lawrence River — Canadians, Québécois, or the Mohawk Indians. The Mohawks have held the title for years, because of their superior experience with the river's currents while smuggling Canadian cigarettes into the U.S. The natives, secretly financed by the Ontario tobacco growers, can afford modern weapons. Ottawa and Quebec City hastily retrieve cannons from their local museums.

The Canadian civil war is short-lived because the U.S. quickly intervenes on grounds that its national security is dependent on a reliable source of maple syrup. (The powerful IHOP, International House of Pancakes, is suspected of putting pressure on the White

House, whose Texas-born president enjoys his morning stack of flapjacks.)

Canada's other conceivable civil war is caused by *western alienation*. This term does not refer to B.C.'s having more aliens than Ottawa. It means that, in sharing the bounty of this great land, the West Coast people feel that they are sucking the hind teat. They see an advantage in joining the western states of America. Linking Alaska and Washington as one majestic oil pipeline. Changing the name of British Columbia to Cascadia, or possibly Upper Disneyland.

This war of secession will stem from the West's perception of Central Canada, now viewed in much the same way that the starving Armenians regarded Central Russia.

It's the tyranny of Toronto.

Western Americans don't mind *their* country's largest city, New York, because Manhattan is more than Wall Street. For western Canadians, however, Toronto is entirely Bay Street. There may be a few other minor lanes running through Toronto, but Bay Street is the main thoroughfare for the seven-days-a-week parade of the Almighty Dollar (sixty-some cents U.S.).

"The centre of the known universe" — that is the westerner's sobriquet for Toronto. When a westerner's life savings are wiped out by a market crash, what does he hold responsible? The Toronto Stock Exchange! That electronically-enhanced Wicked Witch of the East.

Yet, and despite these strong feelings of persecution, the West is unlikely to take up arms to separate from Central Canada. To do so would complicate the tourist trade. European visitors might balk at having to duck mortar shells in order to visit Stanley Park. More likely, therefore, is *partial* separation by Vancouver Island. Such a split has worked well for Taiwan, separating from China. The island is more prosperous than the mainland. Which suggests that Victoria could be another Taipei.

The Empress Hotel would never look back. Watch for another Boston Tea Party, with crumpets.

Americanada

For Canada's provinces, the whole is not greater than the sum of the parts. The parts are too big to fit into the whole. Each part thinks of itself as an entirety. This makes Canada entirely wrong.

Thus in a crisis, such as a Quebec referendum on separation, the country splits into political segments, in this case PQ and TROC (the Rest of Canada). Like the tail wagging the dog, this being reduced to an appendage irritates the vast majority of Canadians who don't appreciate being remaindered.

So, the easiest way for Canada to get its act together would be for the whole country to become part of the United States of America. This suggestion causes mass swooning in Ottawa, which would need to convert the federal Parliament buildings into rather rococo bowling alleys.

The fact is, however, that Canada is already, to all intents and purposes, an American dominion.

Economically, culturally, and militarily, the U.S. is Us.

When the American economy sneezes, Canada's develops viral pneumonia. The U.S. dollar is the standard by which Canadians judge the value of the loonie. It breeds contempt for our currency. People no longer stoop to pick up a nickel. It's not worth their time. But an American quarter is *cash*. This is why doing a Euro job on the Canadian and American dollars would do wonders for the nation's self-esteem, and the Queen would be glad to get off our penny.

In fact the only Canadians who would lose out financially if the country became an official part of the States would be its politicians, who would have to adapt to being smaller frogs in a big pond. If not actual pond scum.

Canadian politicians — none of whom could realistically aspire to becoming president of the United States — can therefore be expected to object loudly to such an American blending. To wrap themselves in the maple leaf and muster a clutch of Scottish pipers to parade in defence of Canadians' distinctive nationality.

This raises the question: *What* distinctive nationality?

Most Canadians would agree that they possess a collective persona that distinguishes them from other nationals. We just have difficulty identifying it in a lineup of peoples.

A lot depends on wearing a Don Cherry collar and jacket. With Don Cherry in them.

God's frozen people. That is how much of the world views the inhabitants of "our home and native land." (And having "native land" enshrined in the national anthem doesn't help in defending against the aboriginal claim to the choicer lots.)

Aside from the refrigerated image, reflected in their politics, Canadians are generally less patriotic than

Voter

Americans. The Yanks do not hesitate to die for their country, whereas Canucks would like to discuss it first.

Canadians limit bumptious nationalism to TV beer commercials ("I *am* Canadian!"). While the American icons are generals Grant and Lee, the Canadian are Molson and Labatt.

One is the home of "the free and the brave," the other the land of the brew and the zed (not zee).

Also, the American eagle, as a national symbol, clearly outranks the Canada goose ("Honkey"). Like the goose, in the fall Canadians migrate south in thousands to the warmer climes of Florida and California. They are fair-weather patriots.

In contrast, the American eagle is fiercely territorial. More independent. Self-confident enough to fly alone, at great heights, albeit sometimes in circles.

The Canada goose, however, is more comfortable moving as part of a flock (socialist party). Vee the people. This bird is fixated on the butt of the bird ahead, whereas the eagle — more far-sighted — will dive to pick up a piece of the world's economy before it even realizes that it is prey.

These national distinctions between Canadians and Americans — in addition to the colour problem (color problem) exacerbated by computer word processors designed in the U.S. — make Americanada unlikely.

Also, the Americans are fiercely protective of self-government. They still fear — subconsciously, of course — that if they are not vigilant about political change the country will lapse back into a British colony. Possibly as a result of some invading force like the Spice Girls.

The U.S. narrowly escaped becoming a dominion of the Beatles. John Lennon was assassinated in New York by an American patriot who, though barmy, sensed the threat.

For these reasons, much as Canada might relish marriage as well as intercourse with the States, the Americans would be leery. They know, many of them, that Canada still bows to the monarch, who drives in the same royal coach used by George the Third when he was hiring German mercenaries to come over to his American colonies and get aerated by Minutemen.

Besides which, it is a real comfort for Americans to be able to blame their bad weather on Canada. Not *all* their ill winds, of course. Some of these —hurricanes and the like — blow in from Cuba and other bad influences in the Caribbean. But the blizzard is made in Canada, and guaranteed colder than a witch's teat.

Where Canadian Politicians Come From

"When I grow up, I want to be a politician." How often do we hear this from a child, presuming that the kid has an IQ competitive with that of a kumquat?

Not, one ventures to say, very often.

Compared to the career options of becoming an astronaut or a brain surgeon or even a professional bum, politicking ranks well down among the sleazier callings.

Yet we observe no shortage of politicians. They are one of our few natural resources not threatened with depletion. Canada's record is clean, in regard to clear-cutting politicians — growth that seems to thrive in poor prairie soil as readily as in the soggy climes of both coasts.

To date, genome science has not found a human gene that causes a person to develop into a politician. The phenomenon appears to be related to neither nature nor nurture, but to accidental factors.

Where do politicians come from?

Such as being sucked into a *committee*.

Every committee, even a church committee to raise funds for a new pew, has the potential to engender politics in a person who would normally never think of getting involved in anything riskier than sex or scuba diving.

It is by becoming engaged with a committee that the budding politician gets his first intoxicating taste of being a *chair*. Becoming a committee chair is the political equivalent of losing one's virginity. Instead of being satisfied with stroking one's ego in private, one seeks to dominate other committee members — municipally, provincially, federally — or in Adolf Hitler's case, the world committee.

This scary progression is masked by the neo-politician's self-delusion that he or she is "serving the public." Wrong. Waiters serve the public. Politicians bring nothing to the table but the bill.

Such a politician was the Emperor Caligula, who appointed his horse to the Senate, thereby setting a precedent for nominations to Canada's Upper House. Cal undoubtedly started his career as a chair of some Roman committee, probably to promote equine representation in government.

Aside from chairing, the politician needs no special training. Universities do have departments of political science, but to date none has produced a scientific politician.

Except, that is, for political *physics*. The politician uses people as a power source. To run (for office) he has to be "plugged in" to public sentiment. But he has no specific gravity. In fact, telling jokes is part of his drive for votes. As for his relative density, he tries to keep his family from speaking in public.

Another major source of politicians is the legal profession, as lawyers feel that they can sink no lower in public esteem. Also an asset: a lawyer is able to stand

Electioneering

up and talk at the same time. Ordinary folk need all their concentration to engage in either of these activities, and trying to combine them gives us gas. (Incidentally, the silent fart, so essential in the political forum, is a skill mastered by the lawyer.)

The other traditional lapse into Canadian politics is that of church ministers. There are no atheists in the foxholes or in the legislatures. A belief in the existence of a Supreme Being — other than No. 99 — seems obligatory, if only so that the politician may find comfort in the national anthem ("God keep our land").

Baptist ministers, in the Prairie provinces, have shown the same aptitude as lawyers in haranguing a captive audience. Why Baptist ministers? Why not Anglican, Catholic, Presbyterian, United Church, or the odd Tibetan lama? The answer seems to be that Prairie farmers, often desperate for rain for their crops, hear the Baptist as a watery messiah. In contrast, politicians who were formerly Baptist ministers are much rarer in regions like British Columbia, where there is an abundance of precipitation.

Finally, all aspirants to public office should keep in mind the conclusive judgment brought down by Woody Allen: "Politicians are a notch beneath child molesters."

Rehabilitating the Image

Yes, *something* must be done to glamorize Canada's politics. According to a CBC poll, 98 percent of U.S. residents do not know the name of Canada's prime minister. The other 2 percent made lucky guesses. And the 98 percent includes Canadians who just moved to the States last week.

These stats indicate a grave imbalance of notoriety. Most Canadians know the name of the American president, probably that of his wife as well, and a majority can name his dog. How does Canada's PM gain that kind of recognition, short of getting caught having sex in the Oral Office, House of Commons?

The Yanks have of course no notion whatever of the names of the competing traditional parties in Canada. In the U.S. the Republican Party (GOP) is made easier to remember by its symbol, the elephant. The Democrats, by the donkey. (Mr. Ross Perot's

Image operation

party does not appear to have associated itself with any animal, possibly at the request of the SPCA).

So, what creatures might help Canadian newspaper cartoonists to make this nation's political parties more readily recognized as bestial? Some suggestions:

Conservatives: The moose. Able to look dignified while standing in a swamp. Independent (carries his own coat rack). Bullish, very competitive, especially when in rut. Loud voice, rarely mellifluous.

Liberals: The Canada goose. Very social. Makes a mess if allowed to feed in places used by humans. Highly vocal in flight from reality. Production program: lay an egg.

New Democrats: The rabbit. Lovable but not overly bright. Rarely aggressive by nature. Makes an excellent pet for Big Labour.

Greens: The flounder. Also believes in Cod. Identifies with all threatened species except man.

Scrap the Welfare State

As a result of her politics, Canada is on welfare. This country expects the government to take care of everything except occasional irregularity. From the cradle to the grave, plus some prenatal benefits.

With employment insurance, medicare, and possible postal delivery, are the people not losing the sense of personal responsibility that distinguishes civilized man from the bath sponge? What is happening to rugged individualism, or even flabby individualism?

To find a Canadian who expects nothing from the government, who in fact when offered it, will throw up on one's shoes, one must travel deep into the bush, searching till one hears of a local hermit the Indians call "Crazy George."

Crazy George is old enough to remember when a daycare centre for adults was called "a saloon." He has refused to apply for the old-age pension because it is against his principles to engage in any activity that requires him to produce a document such as his birth

The Golden Future

certificate. Or to be grotesquely photographed for a driver's licence. Or to include GST when selling his soul to the devil.

Crazy George makes a living by the only means that doesn't compromise his independence: stealing. He dreads dying because there is no one to bury him except the government, and they will want him to provide his change of address.

Tell a Canadian to use self-reliance, and he'll ask, "Where do I pick up the application form?" More usefully he should be offered:

Options for Improvement of Canadian Politics:

Anarchism. May be defined as the total rejection of government as a spinal replacement for the individual. Benefit: without government there would be no politicians, immediately improving Canada's air quality.

Needless to say, governments do not approve of anarchists and encourage people to think of the anarchist as a skulking figure in a black cloak under which he carries a round bomb. A false picture, confusing the anarchist with the sexual exhibitionist.

Au contraire, the anarchist is an immoderately civilized idealist who assumes that people are capable of looking after themselves without a SIN. Caring. Socially co-operative. Comfortable with the concept of being personally responsible for their actions. Anarchists are *nice*.

Anyhow, political futurists say that democratic government is becoming increasingly irrelevant because most of the decision-making is done by bureaucrats. This is why, basically, all Canadian governments look and act alike: the bureaucrats tell the politicians that nothing can be changed without damaging the status quo. Thus Parliament Hill comprises geological layers of status quo, which is the hardest substance known to science.

Vox pop

However, enviable though an anarchist society would be, for Canadians it would have its drawbacks. For instance, scores of political cartoonists would be thrown out of work. Almost as serious, several million civil servants would be not only not working, but also unemployed.

Yet the gravest consequence of scrapping public politics in Canada would be that the people would not have the government to blame for everything but black holes in other galaxies. They would, of necessity, have to go back to accusing God. Or, more likely, a

Cabinet of gods: Mammon (Treasury Board), Moloch (Child Welfare), Mars (Defence), Somnus (Senate), etc. But society might boggle at restoring human sacrifice to replace the taxpayer. The bottom line: anarchism is noble but nut-prone.

One-term Office. Under the present system, once a person is elected to office, all his focus and energy are directed towards getting *re-elected.*

This is the major flaw in the present election system: *it permits voters to make the same mistake twice*.

Sir John A's Legacy?

Because they hope to be elected again and again, till they are too frail to run for anything *but* office, politicians now see facing reality as a retirement hobby. They are not encouraged to do what is right rather than what is popular. The members of government set the standard for being politically correct — the rubber rectitude.

In this respect the American system is superior, in that the president is limited to two terms of office or assassination, whichever comes first. By law he is not allowed to just change his name, his underwear, his wife, and try to sneak back into the White House wearing false whiskers.

Military Coup. In Canada the elected government has never become so corrupt that a Canadian army general felt obliged to seize the reins of power on the political merry-go-round.

Would Canadian politics benefit from the occasional coup, provided that it was bloodless and didn't interrupt delivery of pension cheques? Would a Fidel Castro breathe new life into the system of government, especially for guys who hate shaving? Yes, obviously. But it is hard to imagine that any Canadian army general would be megalomaniac enough to want to live in Ottawa.

More Women in Politics. Women have proved to be more honest, courageous, and hard-working, but this is no reason not to have more of them in government.

Q. Why should I pay attention to Canadian politics, when watching it makes me nauseous?

A. Canadians have a duty to other politically oppressed peoples of the world to act as though democracy works.

This role model has for years been provided mostly by the United States of America. But in recent times the American eagle has gone into molt. Under presidents like Nixon, Clinton, and the brambly Bushes, the U.S. system of administration has given new lustre to the reign of Ethelred the Unsteady.

Many emergent democracies now look elsewhere — specifically to Canada — for the example of a system of responsible government that not only avoids the cult of personality but actually overdoes it.

Prematurely aged though politics in Canada may appear, we owe it to billions of people around the globe to prop up the invalid, pinch some colour into his cheeks, and show that there is nothing wrong with our politics that can't be fixed with a quick, bloodless heart transplant.

God save the Queen, and do what He can about Charles!